First Facts®

Staying Safe

Food Safety

by Sally Lee

CAPSTONE PRESS
a capstone imprint

First Facts is published by Capstone Press,
1710 Roe Crest Drive, North Mankato, Minnesota 56003.
www.capstonepub.com

Books published by Capstone Press are manufactured with paper
containing at least 10 percent post-consumer waste.

Library of Congress Cataloging-in-Publication Data
Lee, Sally.
  Food safety / by Sally Lee.
    p. cm. — (First facts. Staying safe)
  Includes bibliographical references and index.
  Summary: "Discusses the rules and techniques for food safety"—Provided by publisher.
  ISBN 978-1-4296-7618-2 (library binding) — ISBN 978-1-4296-7958-9 (paperback)
  1. Food—Juvenile literature. 2. Food—Safety measures—Juvenile literature. I. Title.
  TX355.L368 2012
  363.19′26—dc23   2011021527

Editorial Credits
Christine Peterson, editor; Bobbie Nuytten, designer; Sarah Schuette, photo stylist; Marcy Morin,
    scheduler; Kathy McColley, production specialist

Photo Credits
Capstone Studio: Karon Dubke, cover (main), 1, 5, 7, 8, 11, 13, 14, 17, 18, 20
Shutterstock: Serg64, cover inset (blue sky), zentilia, 6

Consultant: Food Safety Project, Iowa State University Extension and Outreach, Ames, Iowa,
    http://www.iowafoodsafety.org

Essential content terms are **bold** and are defined at the bottom of the spread where
they first appear.

Printed in the United States of America in North Mankato, Minnesota.
112015   009342R

Table of Contents

Food and Bacteria

It's after school, and you're hungry. The turkey sandwich your brother left on the table after lunch looks yummy. But watch out! That sandwich is covered with tiny germs called **bacteria**. Bacteria are everywhere—even inside you. Good bacteria fight off bad germs and help you **digest** food. But harmful bacteria can make food unsafe.

bacteria—very small living things that can cause disease
digest—to break down food so it can be used by the body

What's hiding on your hands? Tiny bacteria and **viruses**, that's what. Bacteria and viruses are on everything you touch. Send those germs down the drain before eating or handling food. Wash your hands with soap and water for 20 seconds. Cover your hands with soap and scrub well.

virus—a germ that copies itself inside the body's cells and can cause disease

Keep It Clean

Harmful bacteria and viruses are sneaky. They hide on dirty cutting boards, **utensils**, and dishes. Use hot soapy water to clean cutting boards, utensils, and dishes after each use. Rinse fruits and vegetables in cool running water. Backpacks carry germs along with books. Keep them off tables and counters where you prepare or eat food.

utensil—a knife, spoon, fork or other tool used to prepare food

Separate Foods

Raw meats, **poultry**, and seafood have many bacteria. Keep these raw foods and their juices away from other foods. At the grocery store, place raw meats, poultry, and seafood in plastic bags. Separate these items from other food in the shopping cart.

poultry—birds that are raised for food

At home, use different cutting boards and utensils for raw meat and other foods. Keep raw meats away from cooked food by using separate, clean plates.

The Right Temperature

Cooking food to a high temperature kills harmful bacteria and makes food safe to eat. Don't eat foods containing raw eggs—not even the cookie dough you like to snitch. Thermometers show when food is cooked to a safe temperature. New bacteria grow as food cools. Eat cooked food while it's hot. Keep foods out of the Temperature Danger Zone (TDZ). Food hits the TDZ when its between 41 and 135 degrees Fahrenheit (5 and 57 degrees Celsius).

Don't Wait, Refrigerate!

Bacteria grow slowly in cold temperatures. At the store, put cold foods into the cart last. After meals, refrigerate cooked foods within two hours. Keep the refrigerator's temperature below 41°F (5°C). Refrigerators slow down bacteria but don't stop them from growing. Eat leftover foods within four days.

Deep Freeze

Food lasts a long time in the freezer. Bacteria can't grow in frozen food. They start growing again as the food **thaws**. Don't thaw frozen food on the counter. Thaw food safely in a refrigerator. You can thaw food in a microwave too. But once food is thawed, it should be cooked and eaten right away.

thaw—to return to a normal temperature after being frozen

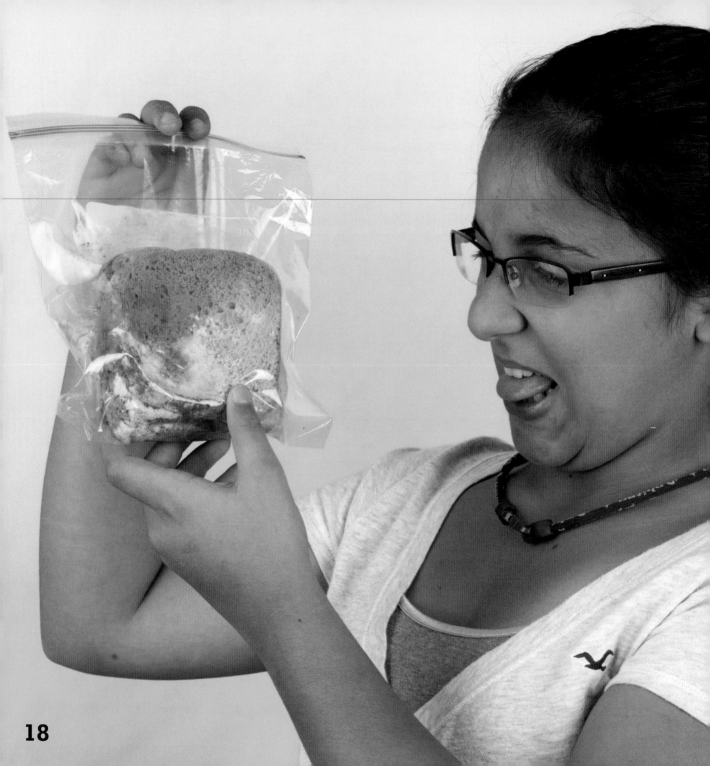

18

Throw It Out

Is there fuzzy **mold** on your food? Does it smell funny? Has it changed color? If so, your food may be unsafe to eat. You can't always tell food is spoiled just by looking at it. But don't taste it. Instead, check the label's **expiration date**. If it's past the date, the food may be unsafe to eat. When in doubt, throw it out.

mold—a fuzzy substance that sometimes grows on old food
expiration date—the last date food should be used

Working Together

Many people work to keep food safe. Farmers follow laws to grow food and raise animals safely. Some government officials make laws to protect your food. Other government workers **inspect** food and the places where it's made and packaged. Stores can sell only safe, inspected food.

inspect—to look at something carefully

Hands On:
How Bacteria Grow

Yeast is not bacteria. But both yeast and bacteria grow faster in some temperatures. Do they grow faster when the temperature is hot, cold, or warm?

What You Need

measuring cup
¼ cup (60 mL) boiling water
3 small bowls
¼ cup (60 mL) ice water

¼ cup (60 mL) warm water
measuring spoons
3 teaspoons (45 mL) sugar
3 packets of dry yeast

What You Do

1. With an adult's help, heat ¼ cup (60 mL) water to boiling in a microwave. Pour boiling water into a bowl.
2. Pour ice water and warm water into separate bowls.
3. Measure and add sugar to each bowl.
4. Stir a packet of yeast into each bowl.
5. Wait for 10 to 15 minutes. The yeast should start to grow. Which bowl of yeast grew the fastest?

Yeast grew quickly in warm water. It grew more slowly in the ice water and boiling water. Temperature affects yeast and bacteria in similar ways. Would bacteria grow faster on food cooking on the stove, in the refrigerator, or sitting on the kitchen counter?

Glossary

bacteria (bak-TEER-ee-uh)—very small living things that exist all around you and inside you; some bacteria cause disease

digest (dy-GEST)—to break down food so it can be used by the body

expiration date (ek-spuh-RAY-shuhn DAYT)—the last date food should be eaten before it is considered spoiled

inspect (in-SPEKT)—to look at something carefully

mold (MOHLD)—a fuzzy substance that sometimes grows on old food

poultry (POHL-tree)—birds that are raised for their eggs and meat; chicken, turkey, ducks, and geese are poultry

thaw (THAW)—to return to a normal temperature after being frozen

utensil (yoo-TEN-sil)—a tool used to eat or prepare food; knives, forks, and spoons are utensils

virus (VYE-russ)—a germ that copies itself inside the body's cells and can cause disease

Read More

Minden, Cecilia. *Keep It Clean: Time to Wash Up.* 21st Century Basic Skills Library Level 1. Ann Arbor, Mich.: Cherry Lake Pub., 2010.

Rau, Dana Meachen. *Food Safety.* Safe Kids. New York: Marshall Cavendish Benchmark, 2009.

Rooke, Thom. *A Germ's Journey.* Follow It! Mankato, Minn.: Picture Window Books, 2011.

Internet Sites

FactHound offers a safe, fun way to find Internet sites related to this book. All of the sites on FactHound have been researched by our staff.

Here's all you do:

Visit *www.facthound.com*

Type in this code: 9781429676182

Super-cool stuff! Check out projects, games and lots more at
www.capstonekids.com

23

Index